For the millennium, to Ellie, with love from Grandma and Grandpa

My Own Story of Jesus
Illustrated by Heinz Giebeler

Contents

Part 1
The Saviour is Born . . . p. 2

Part 2
Jesus and his Friends . . . p. 25

Part 3
Looking and Finding . . . p. 49

Part 4
Jesus is Alive . . . p. 73

CANDLE BOOKS

The Saviour is Born

Contents

An angel foretells John's birth	3	The wise men	12
An angel visits Mary	5	Two dreams	15
Mary visits Elizabeth	6	The killing of the children	17
John the Baptist is born	7	Simeon praises God	18
Jesus is born	8	Anna sees the baby Jesus	19
Angels appear to the shepherds	9	The boy Jesus in the temple	20
The shepherds go to the stable	10	Jesus is baptized	22

An angel foretells John's birth

There was a priest named Zechariah with his wife Elizabeth. Both were good people and loved God but they did not have children. Elizabeth could not have any, and she and Zechariah were already old.

One day Zechariah had to take his turn in the temple service. All at once an angel from the Lord appeared to him and said,

"Don't be afraid, Zechariah! God has heard your prayers. Your wife Elizabeth will have a son, and you must

name him John. He will lead many people in Israel to turn back to the Lord their God."

Zechariah said to the angel, "How will I know this is going to happen?"

The angel answered, "I am Gabriel. You have not believed what I have said. So you will not be able to say a thing until all this happens."

When Zechariah came out of the temple, he could not speak, and the people outside knew he had seen a vision. Soon after that, his wife was expecting a baby.

An angel visits Mary

God sent the angel Gabriel to the town of Nazareth in Galilee with a message for a virgin named Mary. She was engaged to Joseph from the family of King David.

The angel greeted Mary and said, "You are truly blessed! The Lord is with you."

Mary was confused by the angel's words and wondered what they meant. Then the angel told Mary, "Don't be afraid! God is pleased with you, and you will have a son. His name will be Jesus. He will be great and will be called the Son of God Most High."

Mary asked the angel, "How can this happen? I am not married!"

The angel answered, "The Holy Spirit will come down to you, and God's power will come over you. Your relative Elizabeth is also going to have a son, even though she is old. Nothing is impossible for God!"

Mary said, "I am the Lord's servant! Let it happen as you have said." And the angel left her.

Mary visits Elizabeth

Mary hurried to a town in the hill country of Judea. She went into Zechariah's home, where she greeted Elizabeth. Then in a loud voice Elizabeth said to Mary: "God has blessed you more than any other woman!"

Mary said: "With all my heart I praise the Lord, and I am glad because of God my Saviour. God has blessed me. God All-Powerful has done great things for me." Mary stayed with Elizabeth about three months. Then she went back home.

John the Baptist is born

When Elizabeth's son was born, her neighbours and relatives heard how kind the Lord had been to her, and they too were glad.

Eight days later they did for the child what the Law of Moses commands. They were going to name him Zechariah, after his father. Zechariah asked for a writing tablet. Then he wrote, "His name is John." Everyone was amazed. Right away, Zechariah started speaking and praising God.

Jesus is born

About that time, Emperor Augustus gave orders for the names of all the people to be listed in record books. Everyone had to go to their hometown to be listed. Joseph had to leave Nazareth and go to Bethlehem.

Mary was engaged to Joseph and travelled with him. She was soon going to have a baby, and while they were there, she gave birth to her first-born son. She dressed him in baby clothes and laid him on a bed of hay, because there was no room for them in the inn.

Angels appear to the shepherds

That same night in the fields near Bethlehem some shepherds were guarding their sheep. All at once an angel came down to them from the Lord, and the brightness of the Lord's glory flashed around them. The shepherds were frightened. But the angel said, "Don't be afraid! I have good news for you, which will make everyone happy. This very day in King David's hometown a Saviour was born for you. He is Christ the Lord. You will know who he is, because you will find him lying on a bed of hay."

Suddenly many other angels came down from heaven and joined in praising God. They said:

"Praise God in heaven!
Peace on earth to everyone
 who pleases God."

The shepherds go to the stable

After the angels had left and gone back to heaven, the shepherds said to each other, "Let's go to Bethlehem and see what the Lord has told us about." They hurried off and found Mary and Joseph, and they saw the baby lying on a bed of hay.

When the shepherds saw Jesus, they told his parents what the angel had said about him. Everyone listened and was surprised. But Mary kept thinking about all this and wondering what it meant.

As the shepherds returned to their sheep, they were praising God and saying wonderful things about him. Everything they had seen and heard was just as the angel had said.

The wise men

When Jesus was born in Bethlehem, some wise men from the east came to Jerusalem and asked, "Where is the child born to be king of the Jews? We saw his star in the east and have come to worship him."

When King Herod heard about this, he was worried. He brought together the religious leaders and asked them, "Where will the Messiah be born?" They told him, "He will be born in Bethlehem, just as the prophets wrote."

Herod secretly called in the wise men and told them, "Go to Bethlehem and search carefully for the child. As soon as you find him, let me know. I want to go and worship him too."

The wise men listened to what the king said, then left. And the star they had seen in the east went on ahead of them until it stopped over the place where the baby Jesus was. When the men went into the house and saw the child with Mary, his mother, they knelt down and worshipped him. They took out their gifts and gave them to him.

Two dreams

Later, the wise men were warned in a dream not to return to Herod, and they went back home by another road.

After the wise men had gone, an angel from the Lord appeared to Joseph in a dream and said, "Get up! Hurry and take the child and his mother to Egypt! Stay there until I tell you to return, because Herod is looking for the child and wants to kill him."

That night, Joseph got up and took Mary and the baby to Egypt, where they stayed until Herod died.

The killing of the children

When Herod found out that the wise men from the east had tricked him, he was very angry. He gave orders for his men to kill all the boys who lived in or near Bethlehem and were two years old and younger.

Simeon praises God

The time came for Mary and Joseph to do what the Law of Moses says a mother is supposed to do after her baby is born.

At this time a man named Simeon was living in Jerusalem. He was a good man and loved God.

Simeon took the baby Jesus in his arms and praised God, "Lord, now I can die in peace, because you have kept your promise to me. With my own eyes I have seen what you have done to save your people."

Anna sees the baby Jesus

The prophet Anna was also there in the temple. She was eighty-four years old. Night and day she served God by praying and often going without eating.

At that time Anna came and praised God. She spoke about the child Jesus to everyone who hoped for Jerusalem to be set free.

After that, Joseph and Mary returned home to Nazareth. The child Jesus grew. He became strong and wise, and God blessed him.

The boy Jesus in the temple

Every year Jesus' parents went to Jerusalem for the festival of Passover. And when Jesus was twelve years old, they all went there as usual for the celebration. After Passover his parents left, but they did not know that Jesus had stayed on in the city. They thought he was travelling with some other people, and they went a whole day before they started looking for him. When they could not find him, they went back to Jerusalem and started looking for him there.

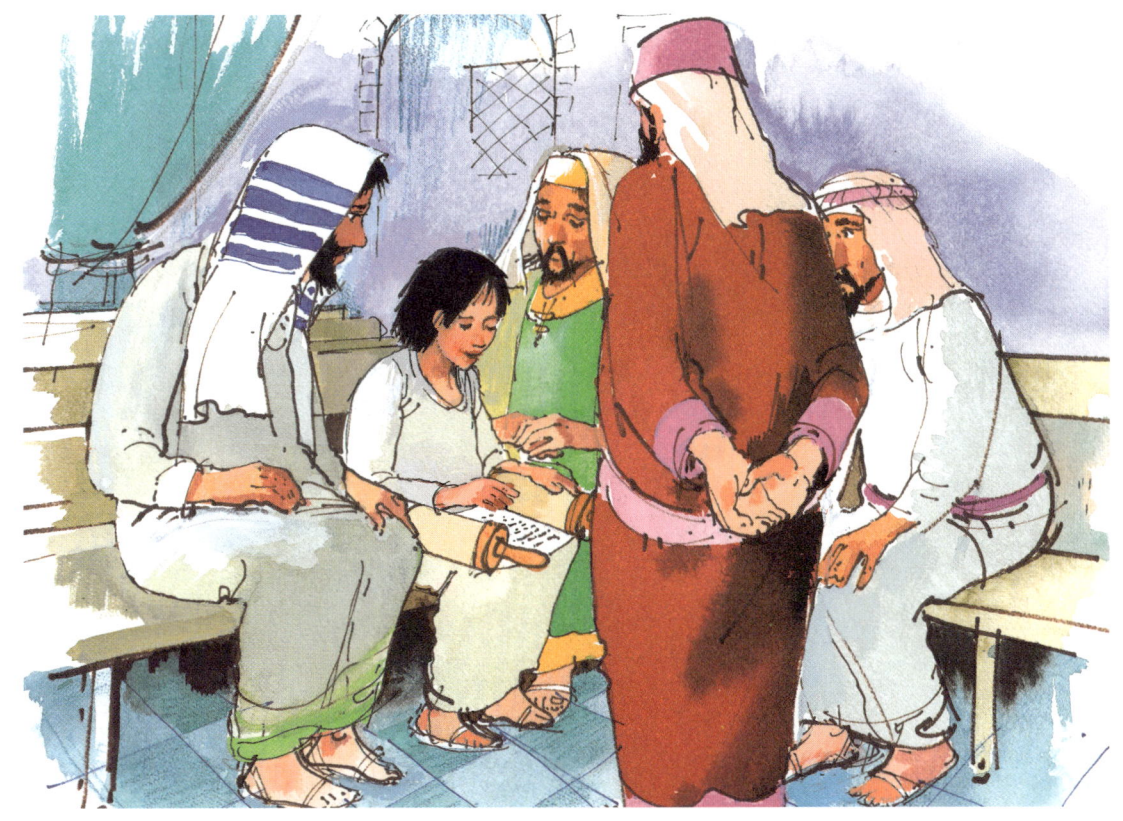

Three days later they found Jesus sitting in the temple, listening to the teachers and asking them questions.

His parents were amazed and his mother said, "Son, why have you done this to us? Your father and I have been very worried, and we have been searching for you!"

Jesus answered, "Didn't you know that I would be in my Father's house?"

Jesus went back to Nazareth with his parents and obeyed them. His mother kept on thinking about all that had happened.

Jesus is baptized

Years later, John the Baptist started preaching in the desert of Judea. He said, "Turn back to God! The kingdom of heaven will soon be here."

John wore clothes made of camel's hair. He had a leather strap around his waist and ate grasshoppers and wild honey.

From Jerusalem and all Judea and from the Jordan River Valley crowds of people went to John. They told how sorry they were for their sins, and he baptized them in the river.

John said, "I baptize you with water so that you will give up your sins. But someone more powerful is going to come, and I am not good enough even to carry his sandals. He will baptize you with the Holy Spirit."

Jesus left Galilee and went to the Jordan River to be baptized by John. But John kept objecting and said, "I ought to be baptized by you. Why have you come to me?"

Jesus answered, "For now this is how it should be, because we must do all that God wants us to do."

So Jesus was baptized. As soon as he came out of the water, the sky opened, and he saw the Spirit of God coming down on him like a dove. Then a voice from heaven said, "This is my own dear Son; I am pleased with him."

You can find these stories in your Bible

An angel foretells John's birth	*Luke 1:5-25*
An angel visits Mary	*Luke 1:26-38*
Mary visits Elizabeth	*Luke 1:39-56*
John the Baptist is born	*Luke 1:57-80*
Jesus is born	*Luke 2:1-7*
Angels appear to the shepherds	*Luke 2:8-14*
The shepherds go to the stable	*Luke 2:15-20*
The wise men	*Matthew 2:1-8*
Two dreams	*Matthew 2:9-15*
The killing of the children	*Matthew 2:16-18*
Simeon praises God	*Luke 2:21-40*
Anna sees the baby Jesus	*Luke 2:36-38*
The boy Jesus in the temple	*Luke 2:41-52*
Jesus is baptized	*Matthew 3:1-17*

Jesus and his Friends

Jesus and his Friends

Contents

The young fishermen	27	Zacchaeus the tax-collector	40
Two sick people	30	Peter sinks	43
The paralyzed man	34	Blind Bartimaeus	46
The crippled woman	37		

The young fishermen

One day, Jesus was standing on the shore of Lake Galilee, teaching the people as they crowded around him to hear God's message. Near the shore he saw two boats left there by some fishermen who had gone to wash their nets. Jesus got into the boat that belonged to Simon and asked him to row it out a little way from the shore. Then Jesus sat sown in the boat to teach the crowd.

When Jesus had finished speaking, he told Simon, "Row the boat out into the deep water and let your nets down to catch some fish."

"Master," Simon answered, "we have worked hard all night long and have not caught a thing. But if you tell me to, I will let the nets down."

They did it and caught so many fish that their nets began ripping apart. Then they signalled for their partners in the other boat to come and help them. Together they filled the two boats so full that they began to sink.

When Simon Peter saw this happen, he knelt down in front of Jesus and said, "Lord, don't come near me! I am a sinner." Peter and everyone with him were completely surprised at all the fish they had caught. His partners James and John, the sons of Zebedee, were surprised too.

Jesus told Simon, "Don't be afraid! From now on you will bring in people instead of fish." The men pulled their boats up on the shore. Then they left everything and went with Jesus.

Two sick people

Once again a large crowd gathered around Jesus. A man called Jairus went over to him. He knelt at Jesus' feet and started begging for help. He said, "My daughter is about to die! Please come and touch her, so she will get well."

Jesus went with Jairus. Many people followed along, crowding around.

In the crowd was a woman who had been bleeding for twelve years. She had gone to many doctors, and paid them all the money she had. But instead of getting better, she only got worse.

The woman had said to herself, "If I can just touch Jesus' clothes, I will get well." As soon as she touched them, her bleeding stopped, and she knew she was well.

At that moment Jesus felt power go out of him. He turned to the crowd and asked, "Who touched my clothes?"

His disciples said to him, "Look at all these people crowding around you! How can you ask who touched you?"

The woman came shaking with fear and knelt down in front of Jesus. Then she told him the whole story.

Jesus said to the woman, "You are now well because of your faith. May God give you peace!"

While Jesus was still speaking, some men came from Jairus' home and said, "Your daughter has died!" Jesus said to Jairus, "Don't worry. Just have faith!"

Jesus did not let anyone go with him to Jairus' home except Peter and the two brothers, James and John. They saw the people crying and

making a lot of noise. Then Jesus went inside and said to them, "Why are you crying and carrying on like this? The child isn't dead. She is just asleep." But the people laughed at him.

Jesus took the girl's father and mother and his three disciples and went to where she was. He took the twelve-year-old girl by the hand and said, "Little girl, get up!" The girl got right up and started walking around.

Everyone was greatly surprised.

The paralyzed man

Jesus went back to Capernaum, and a few days later people heard that he was at home. Then so many of them came to the house that there wasn't even standing room left in front of the door.

Jesus was still teaching when four people came up, carrying a paralyzed man on a mat. But because of the crowd, they could not get him to Jesus. So they made a hole in the roof above him and let the man down in front of everyone.

When Jesus saw how much faith they had, he said to the crippled man, "My friend, your sins are forgiven."

Some of the religious leaders there started wondering, "Why would he say such a thing? He must think he is God! Only God can forgive sins."

Right away, Jesus knew what they were thinking, and he said, "Why are you thinking such things? Is it easier for me to tell this paralyzed man that his sins are forgiven or to tell him to get up and pick up his mat and go on home? I will show you that I have the right to forgive sins here on earth." So Jesus said to the man, "Get up! Pick up your mat and go on home."

The man got right up. He picked up his mat and went out while everyone watched in amazement. They praised God and said, "We have never seen anything like this."

The crippled woman

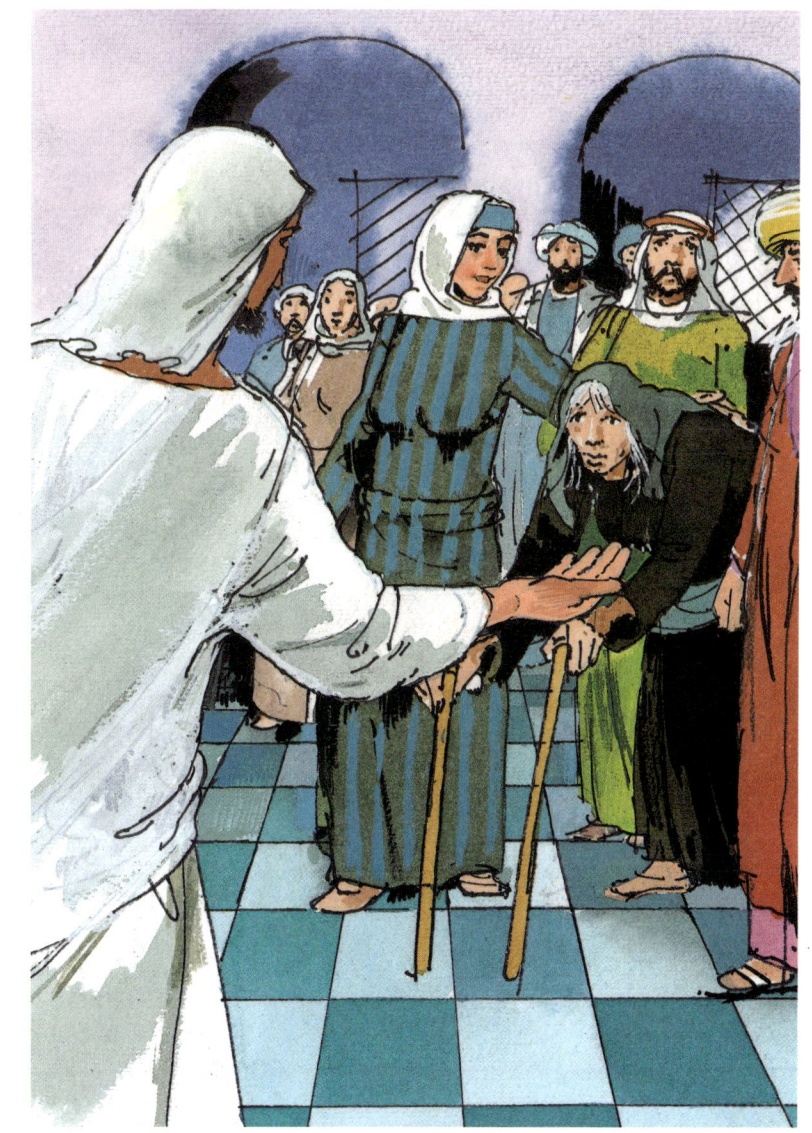

One Sabbath, Jesus was teaching in a Jewish meeting place, and a woman was there who had been crippled for eighteen years. She was completely bent over and could not straighten up. When Jesus saw the woman, he called her over and said, "You are now well." He placed his hands on her, and right away she stood up straight and praised God.

The man in charge of the meeting place was angry because Jesus had healed someone on the Sabbath. So he said to the people, "Each week has six days when we can work. Come and be healed on one of those days, but not on the Sabbath."

Jesus replied, "Are you trying to fool someone? Won't any one of you untie your ox or donkey and lead it out to drink on a Sabbath? Isn't it right to set this crippled woman free on the Sabbath?"

Jesus' words made his enemies ashamed. But everyone else in the crowd was happy about the wonderful things he was doing.

Zacchaeus the tax-collector

Jesus was going through Jericho, where a man named Zacchaeus lived. He was in charge of collecting taxes and was very rich. Jesus was heading his way, and Zacchaeus wanted to see what he was like. But Zacchaeus was a short man and could not see over the crowd. So he ran ahead and climbed up into a sycamore tree.

When Jesus got there, he looked up and said, "Zacchaeus, hurry down! I want to stay with you today." Zacchaeus hurried down and gladly welcomed Jesus.

Everyone who saw this started grumbling, "This man Zacchaeus is a sinner! And Jesus is going home to eat with him."

Later that day Zacchaeus stood up and said to the Lord, "I will give half of my property to the poor, and I will now pay back four times as much to everyone I have ever cheated."

Jesus said to Zacchaeus, "Today you and your family have been saved, because you are truly one of God's special people. I came to look for and to save people who are lost."

Peter sinks

One day Jesus and his disciples spent time on the east side of Lake Galilee. Towards evening he sent the disciples back across the lake in a boat while he went up on a mountain to be alone and pray.

A strong wind arose on the lake and the boat was being tossed around by the waves. By this time the boat was a long way from the shore.

A little while before morning, Jesus came walking on the water toward his disciples. When they saw him, they thought he was a ghost. They were terrified and started screaming.

At once, Jesus said, "Don't worry! I am Jesus. Don't be afraid."

Peter replied, "Lord, if it is really you, tell me to come to you on the water."

"Come on!" Jesus said. Peter then got out of the boat and started walking on the water toward him.

But when Peter saw how strong the wind was, he was afraid and started sinking. "Save me, Lord!" he shouted.

Right away, Jesus reached out his hand. He helped Peter up and said, "You surely don't have much faith. Why do you doubt?"

When Jesus and Peter got into the boat, the wind died down. The men in the boat worshipped Jesus and said, "You really are the Son of God!"

45

Blind Bartimaeus

Jesus and his disciples went to Jericho, and as they were leaving, they were followed by a large crowd. A blind beggar by the name of Bartimaeus was sitting beside the road.

When he heard that it was Jesus, he shouted, "Jesus, have pity on me!"

Many people told the man to stop, but he shouted even louder.

Jesus stopped and said, "Call him over!"

They called out to the blind man and said, "Don't be afraid! Come on! He is calling for you." The man threw off his coat as he jumped up and ran to Jesus.

Jesus asked, "What do you want me to do for you?" The blind man answered, "Master, I want to see!"

Jesus said, "You may go. Your eyes are healed because of your faith."

Right away the man could see, and he went down the road with Jesus.

You can find these stories in your Bible

The young fishermen	*Luke 5:1-11*
Two sick people	*Mark 5:21-43*
The paralyzed man	*Mark 2:1-12*
The crippled woman	*Luke 13:10-17*
Zacchaeus the tax-collector	*Luke 19:1-10*
Peter sinks	*Matthew 14:22-33*
Blind Bartimaeus	*Mark 10:46-52*

Looking and Finding

Looking and Finding

When crowds gathered to hear Jesus teach, he often told them stories called parables. These were tales of every-day life – about farmers or housewives – but they had a spiritual meaning. Here are some of these stories.

Contents

The lost sheep	52
The lost coin	54
The lost son	57
The great banquet	63
The hidden treasure	67
The two house builders	69

Tax collectors and sinners were all crowding around to listen to Jesus. So the Pharisees and the teachers of the Law of Moses started grumbling, "This man is friendly with sinners. He even eats with them."

So Jesus told them this story:

51

The lost sheep

    If any of you has a hundred sheep, and one of them gets lost, what will you do? Won't you leave the ninety-nine in the field and go look for the lost sheep until you find it? And when you find it, you will be so glad that you will put it on your shoulder and carry it home. Then you will call in your friends and neighbours and say, "Let's celebrate! I've found my lost sheep."

Jesus said, "In the same way there is more happiness in heaven because of one sinner who turns to God than over ninety-nine good people who don't need to."

The lost coin

Jesus told the people another story: What will a woman do if she has ten silver coins and loses one of them?

Won't she light a lamp, sweep the floor,
and look carefully until she finds it?

Then she will call in her friends and neighbours and say, "Let's celebrate! I've found the coin I lost."

Jesus said, "In the same way God's angels are happy when even one person turns to him."

The lost son

Jesus also told another story:

Once a man had two sons. The younger son said to his father, "Give me my share of the property."

So the father divided his property between his two sons.

The younger son packed up everything he owned and left for a foreign country, where he wasted all his money.

He had spent everything, when a bad famine spread through that whole land. Soon he had nothing to eat.

He went to work for a man in that country, and the man sent him out to take care of his pigs. He would have been glad to eat what the pigs were eating, but no one gave him a thing.

Finally, he came to his senses and said, "My father's workers have plenty to eat, and here I am, starving to death! I will go to my father and say to him, 'Father, I have sinned against God in heaven and against you. I am no longer good enough to be called your son. Treat me like one of your workers.'"

So the younger son got up and started back to his father. But when he was still a long way off, his father saw him and felt sorry for him. He ran to his son and hugged and kissed him.

The son said, "Father, I have sinned against God in heaven and against you. I am no longer good enough to be called your son."

But his father said to the servants, "Hurry and bring the best clothes and put them on him. Give him a ring for his finger and sandals for his feet. Get the best calf and prepare it, so we can eat and celebrate. This son of mine was dead, but has now come back to life. He was lost and has now been found." And they began to celebrate.

The older son had been out in the field. When he came near the house, he called one of his servants over and asked, "What's going on here?"

The servant told him. The older brother got angry and said to his father, "For years I have worked for you but you have never even given me a little goat, so that I could give a dinner for my friends. This other son of yours wasted your money. Now that he has come home, you order a feast."

His father replied, "My son, you are always with me, and everything I have is yours. But we should be glad and celebrate! Your brother was dead, but he is now alive. He was lost and has now been found."

The great banquet

Jesus told another story:

A man once gave a great banquet and invited a lot of guests. When the banquet was ready, he sent a servant to tell the guests, "Everything is ready! Please come."

One guest after another started making excuses. The first one said, "I bought some land, and I've got to look it over. Please excuse me."

Another guest said, "I bought five teams of oxen, and I need to try them out. Please excuse me."

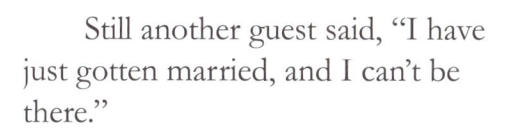

Still another guest said, "I have just gotten married, and I can't be there."

The servant told his master what happened, and the master became so angry that he said,

65

"Go as fast as you can to every street and alley in town! Bring in everyone who is poor or crippled or blind or lame."

When the servant returned, he said, "Master, I've done what you told me, and there is still plenty of room for more people."

His master then told him, "Go out along the country roads and lanes and make people come in, so that my house will be full. Not one of the guests I first invited will get even a bite of my food!"

The hidden treasure

Jesus told this story to show what it is like for people who belong to God's kingdom:

The kingdom of heaven is like what happens when someone finds treasure hidden in a field and buries it again.

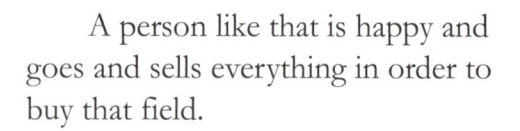

A person like that is happy and goes and sells everything in order to buy that field.

The two house builders

On one occasion Jesus said to the people:

Anyone who hears and obeys these teachings of mine is like a wise person who built a house on solid rock.

Rain poured down, rivers flooded, and winds beat against that house. But it did not fall, because it was built on solid rock.

Anyone who hears my teachings and doesn't obey them is like a foolish person who built a house on sand.

The rain poured down, the rivers flooded, and the winds blew and beat against that house. Finally, it fell with a crash.

You can find these stories in your Bible

The lost sheep	*Luke 15:1-7*
The lost coin	*Luke 15:8-10*
The lost son	*Luke 15:11-32*
The great banquet	*Luke 14:16-24*
The hidden treasure	*Matthew 13:44*
The two house builders	*Matthew 7:24-27*

Jesus is Alive

Jesus is Alive

Contents

Jesus enters Jerusalem	75
Jesus in the temple	76
Jesus is anointed	77
A plot to kill Jesus	78
A special meal with Jesus	79
Jesus prays in Gethsemane	80
Jesus is betrayed and arrested	80
Jesus is put on trial	83
Peter denies Jesus	84
Jesus is tried by Pilate	85
The soldiers make fun of Jesus	80
Jesus is nailed to a cross	87
Jesus dies	88
Jesus is buried	89
Jesus is alive again	90
Jesus appears to Mary	91
Jesus walks to Emmaus	92
Jesus and Thomas	94
Jesus returns to heaven	95

Jesus enters Jerusalem

Jesus and his disciples were on their way to Jerusalem. When they were getting close, Jesus sent two of them on ahead. He told them, "Go into the next village. As soon as you enter it, you will find a young donkey that has never been ridden. Untie the donkey and bring it here."

The disciples left and found the donkey tied near a door that faced the street.

They led the donkey to Jesus. They put some of their clothes on its back, and Jesus got on. Many people spread clothes on the road while others went to cut branches from the fields.

In front of Jesus and behind him, people went along shouting,
"Hooray!
God bless the one who comes in the name of the Lord!
Hooray for God in heaven above!"

Jesus in the temple

After Jesus and his disciples reached Jerusalem, he went into the temple and began chasing out everyone who was selling and buying. He turned over the tables of the money-changers and the benches of those who were selling doves.

Then he taught the people and said, "The Scriptures say, 'My house should be called a place of worship for all nations.' But you have made it a place where robbers hide!"

The religious leaders heard what Jesus said, and they started looking for a way to kill him. They were afraid of him, because the crowds were completely amazed at his teaching.

Jesus is anointed

Jesus was eating in Bethany at the home of Simon, who once had leprosy, when a woman came in with a very expensive bottle of sweet-smelling perfume. After breaking it open, she poured the perfume on Jesus' head. This made some of the guests angry, and they complained, "Why such a waste? We could have sold this perfume for more than three hundred silver coins and given the money to the poor!" So they started saying cruel things to the woman.

But Jesus said: "Leave her alone! Why are you bothering her? She has done a beautiful thing for me. You will always have the poor with you. And whenever you want to, you can give to them. But you won't always have me here with you. You may be sure that wherever the good news is told all over the world, people will remember what she has done. And they will tell others."

A plot to kill Jesus

Judas Iscariot was one of the twelve disciples. He went to the chief priests and offered to help them arrest Jesus. They were glad to hear this, and they promised to pay him. So Judas started looking for a good chance to betray Jesus.

A special meal with Jesus

The night before he was killed, Jesus and his disciples were eating a very special meal together, called the Passover. During the meal Jesus said, "The one who will betray me is now eating with me."

This made the disciples sad, and one after another they said to Jesus, "You surely don't mean me!"

He answered, "It is one of you twelve men who is eating from this dish with me."

While they were eating Jesus took some bread in his hands. He blessed the bread and broke it. Then he gave it to his disciples, and said, "Take this. It is my body."

Jesus picked up a cup of wine and gave thanks to God. He gave it to his disciples, and they all drank some. Then he said, "This is my blood, which is poured out for many people, and with it God makes his agreement."

Jesus prays in Gethsemane

Following the Passover meal, Jesus and his disciples sang a hymn.

Then they went out to the Mount of Olives. They came to a place called Gethsemane, and he told them, "Sit here while I go to pray."

Jesus took along Peter, James, and John. He was sad and troubled and told them, "I am so sad that I feel as if I am dying. Stay here and keep awake with me."

Jesus walked on a little way. Then he knelt down on the ground and prayed, "Father, if it is possible, don't let this happen to me! Father, you can do anything. But do what you want, and not what I want."

When Jesus came back and found the disciples sleeping, he said to Simon Peter, "Are you asleep? Can't you stay awake for just one hour? Stay awake and pray that you won't be tested. You want to do what is right, but you are weak."

Jesus went back and prayed the same prayer. But when he returned to the disciples, he found them sleeping again. They simply could not keep their eyes open, and they did not know what to say.

When Jesus returned to the disciples the third time, he said, "Are you still sleeping and resting? Get up! Let's go. The one who will betray me is already here."

81

Jesus is betrayed and arrested

Jesus was still speaking, when Judas the betrayer came up. He was one of the twelve disciples, and a mob of men armed with swords and clubs were with him.

Judas had told them ahead of time, "Arrest the man I greet with a kiss."

Judas walked right up to Jesus and said, "Teacher!" Then Judas kissed him, and the men grabbed Jesus and arrested him.

Jesus is put on trial

Jesus was led off to the high priest and all the religious leaders met together. They tried to find someone to accuse Jesus of a crime, so they could put him to death. Many people did tell lies, but they did not agree on what they said.

Finally the high priest stood up and asked Jesus, "Are you the Son of God?"

"Yes, I am!" Jesus answered.

At once the high priest ripped his robe apart and shouted, "You heard him claim to be God!" They all agreed that he should be put to death.

Peter denies Jesus

Peter had followed at a distance as Jesus was being led away and he was now in the courtyard of the high priest's house. A servant girl saw Peter warming himself by the fire. She stared at him and said, "You were with Jesus!"

Peter replied, "That isn't true! I don't know what you're talking about." He went out to the gate, and a rooster crowed.

The servant girl saw Peter again and said to the people standing there, "This man is one of them!"

"No, I'm not!" Peter replied.

A little while later some of the people said to Peter, "You certainly are one of them. You're a Galilean!"

This time Peter began to curse and swear, "I don't even know the man you're talking about!"

Right away the rooster crowed a second time. Then Peter remembered that Jesus had told him, "Before a rooster crows twice, you will say three times that you don't know me." So Peter started crying.

Jesus is tried by Pilate

Early the next morning the religious leaders met together. They tied up Jesus and led him off to Pilate. He asked Jesus, "Are you the king of the Jews?"

"Yes," Jesus answered.

The chief priests brought many charges against Jesus. Then Pilate questioned him again, "Don't you have anything to say?" But Jesus did not answer, and Pilate was amazed.

During Passover, Pilate always freed one prisoner. At that time there was a prisoner named Barabbas, who had been arrested for murder. So when the people came and asked Pilate to set a prisoner free, he said, "Do you want me to free the king of the Jews?" But the chief priests told the crowd to ask Pilate to free Barabbas.

Pilate asked the crowd, "What do you want me to do with Jesus?"

They yelled, "Nail him to a cross!"

Pilate wanted to please the crowd. So he ordered his soldiers to beat Jesus with a whip and nail him to a cross.

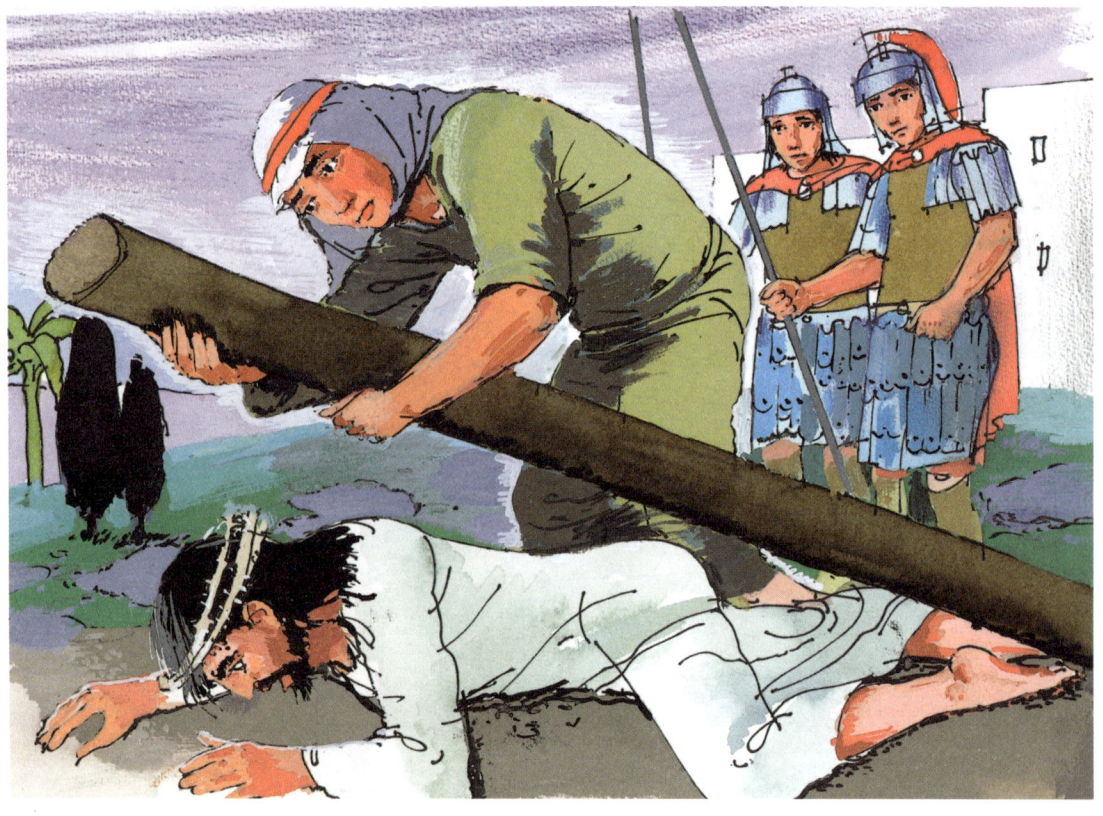

The soldiers make fun of Jesus

The soldiers put a purple robe on Jesus, and on his head they placed a crown that they had made out of thorn branches. They made fun of Jesus and shouted, "Hey, you king of the Jews!" Then they beat him on the head with a stick. They spit on him and knelt down and pretended to worship him.

Then the soldiers took off the purple robe. They put his own clothes back on him and led him off to be nailed to a cross. They forced a passerby named Simon to carry Jesus' cross.

Jesus is nailed to a cross

The soldiers took Jesus to a place named Golgotha, which means "Place of the Skull."

There the soldiers nailed Jesus to a cross and gambled to see who would get his clothes.

The soldiers also nailed two criminals on crosses, one to the right of Jesus and the other to his left.

People who passed by said terrible things about Jesus. They shook their heads and shouted, "Ha! So you're the one who claimed you could tear down the temple and build it again in three days. Save yourself and come down from the cross!"

The religious leaders also made fun of Jesus. They said to each other, "He saved others, but he can't save himself. If he is the king of Israel, let him come down from the cross! Then we will see and believe."

The two criminals also said cruel things to Jesus.

Jesus dies

About noon the sky turned dark and stayed that way until around three o'clock. Then about that time Jesus shouted, "My God, my God, why have you deserted me?"

One of the people standing there ran and grabbed a sponge. After he had soaked it in wine, he put it on a stick and held it up to Jesus.

Jesus shouted again and then died.

A Roman army officer was standing in front of Jesus. When he saw how Jesus died, he said, "This man really was the Son of God!"

Some women were looking on from a distance. They had come with Jesus to Jerusalem.

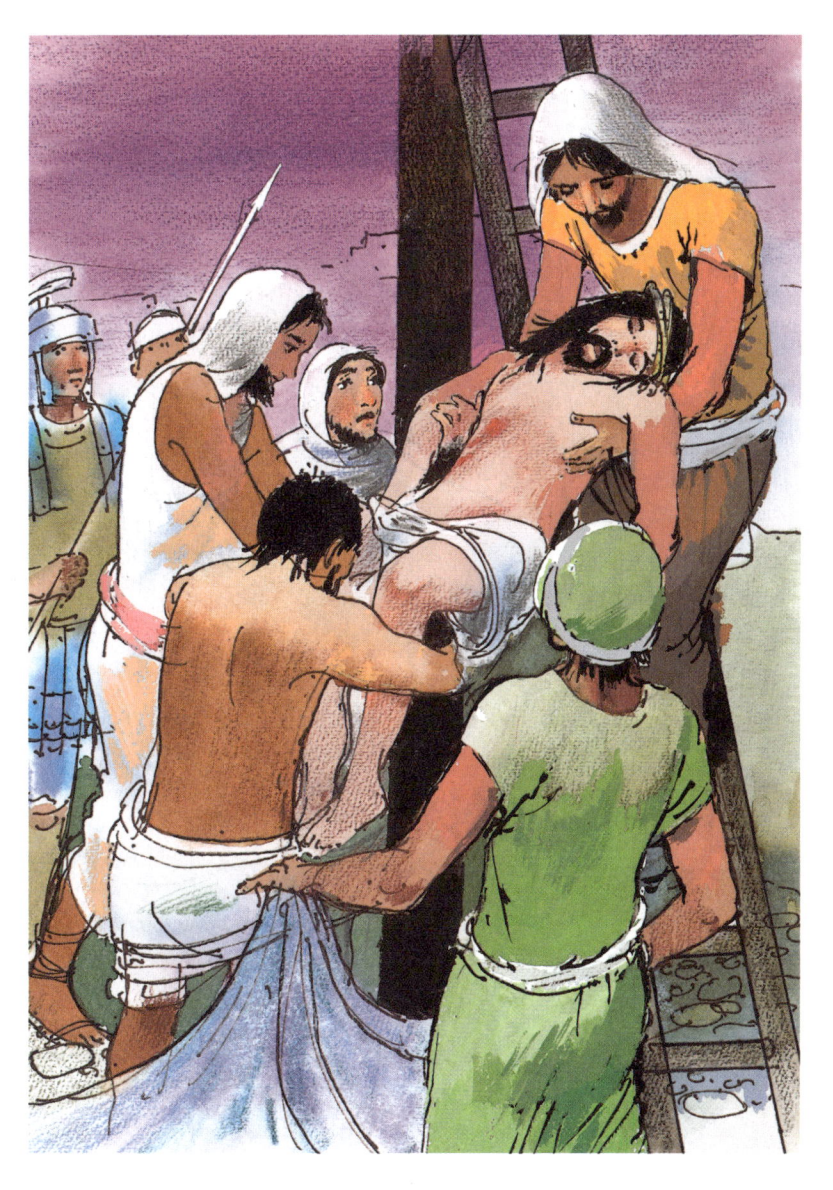

Jesus is buried

A man named Joseph from Arimathea was brave enough to ask Pilate for the body of Jesus.

Pilate called in the army officer to find out if Jesus had been dead very long. After the officer told him, Pilate let Joseph have Jesus' body.

Joseph bought a linen cloth and took the body down from the cross. He had it wrapped in the cloth, and he put it in a tomb that had been cut into solid rock. Then he rolled a big stone against the entrance to the tomb.

89

Jesus is alive again

On Sunday morning while it was still dark, Mary Magdalene went to the tomb and saw that the stone had been rolled away from the entrance. She ran to Simon Peter and to John and said, "They have taken the Lord from the tomb! We don't know where they have put him."

Peter and John started for the tomb. They ran side by side, until John ran faster than Peter and got there first. He bent over and saw the strips of linen cloth lying inside the tomb, but he did not go in.

When Simon Peter got there, he went into the tomb and saw the strips of cloth. He also saw the piece of cloth that had been used to cover Jesus' face. It was rolled up and in a place by itself.

John then went into the tomb, and when he saw everything, he believed that God had raised Jesus from death, just as Scriptures said.

Jesus appears to Mary

Mary Magdalene stood crying outside the tomb. She was still weeping, when she stooped down and saw two angels inside. They were dressed in white and were sitting where Jesus' body had been. One was at the head and the other was at the foot. The angels asked Mary, "Why are you crying?"

She answered, "They have taken away my Lord's body! I don't know where they have put him."

As soon as Mary said this, she turned around and saw Jesus standing there. But she did not know who he was. Jesus asked her, "Why are you crying? Who are you looking for?"

She thought he was the gardener and said, "Sir, if you have taken his body away, please tell me, so I can go and get him."

Then Jesus said to her, "Mary!" She turned and said to him, "Teacher!"

Mary Magdalene then went and told the disciples that she had seen the Lord.

Jesus walks to Emmaus

That same day two of Jesus' disciples were going to the village of Emmaus, which was about seven miles from Jerusalem. As they were talking and thinking about what had happened, Jesus came near and started walking along beside them. But they did not know who he was.

Jesus asked them, "What were you talking about as you walked along?"

The two of them stood there looking sad and gloomy. Then the one named Cleopas asked Jesus, "Are you the only person from Jerusalem who doesn't know what has been happening there these last few days?"

"What do you mean?" Jesus asked.

They answered: "Those things that happened to Jesus from Nazareth. The chief priests and our leaders had him arrested and sentenced to die on a cross. It has already been three days since all this happened. Some women in our group surprised us. They had gone to the tomb early in the morning, but did not find the body of Jesus."

Then Jesus asked the two disciples, "Why can't you understand? How can you be so slow to believe all that the prophets said?"

Jesus then explained everything written about himself in the Scriptures.

When the two of them came near the village where they were going, Jesus seemed to be going farther. They begged him, "Stay with us! It's already late, and the sun is going down." So Jesus went into the house to stay with them.

After Jesus sat down to eat, he took some bread. He blessed it and broke it. Then he gave it to them. At once they knew who he was, but he disappeared. They said to each other, "When he talked with us along the road and explained the Scriptures to us, didn't it warm our hearts?" So they got right up and returned to Jerusalem.

The two disciples found the eleven apostles and the others gathered together. And they learned from the group that the Lord was really alive.

Jesus and Thomas

The disciples locked themselves in a room from fear of the religious leaders. Suddenly, Jesus appeared, greeted them and showed them his hands and his side. When the disciples saw the Lord, they became very happy.

Thomas wasn't with the others when Jesus appeared to them. So they told him, "We have seen the Lord!" But Thomas said, "First, I must see the nail scars in his hands and touch them with my finger. I must put my hand where the spear went into his side. I won't believe unless I do this!"

A week later the disciples were together again. This time, Thomas was with them. Jesus came in, greeted his disciples and said to Thomas, "Put your finger here and look at my hands! Put your hand into my side. Stop doubting and have faith." Thomas replied, "You are my Lord and my God!"

Jesus said, "Do you have faith because you have seen me? The people who have faith in me without seeing me are the ones who are really blessed!"

Jesus returns to heaven

Jesus led his disciples out to Bethany, where he raised his hands and blessed them. As he was doing this, he left and was taken up to heaven. After his disciples had worshipped him, they returned to Jerusalem and were very happy.

They spent their time in the temple, praising God.

You can find these stories in your Bible

Jesus enters Jerusalem	*Mark 11:1-11*
Jesus in the temple	*Mark 11:15-18*
Jesus is anointed	*Mark 14:3-9*
A plot to kill Jesus	*Mark 14:10-16*
A special meal with Jesus	*Mark 14:17-26*
Jesus prays in Gethsemane	*Mark 14:27-42*
Jesus is betrayed and arrested	*Mark 14:43-50*
Jesus is put on trial	*Mark 14:53-64*
Peter denies Jesus	*Mark 14:66-72*
Jesus is tried by Pilate	*Mark 15:1-15*
The soldiers make fun of Jesus	*Mark 15:16-21*
Jesus is nailed to a cross	*Mark 15:22-32*
Jesus dies	*Mark 15:33-41*
Jesus is buried	*Mark 15:42-47*
Jesus is alive again	*John 20:1-10*
Jesus appears to Mary	*John 20:11-18*
Jesus walks to Emmaus	*Luke 24: 13-35*
Jesus and Thomas	*John 20:19-29*
Jesus returns to heaven	*Luke 24:50-53*

Copyright ©1997
Three's Company / Angus Hudson Ltd.
Illustrations copyright ©1991, 1993,
1994 Deutsche Bibelgesellschaft
Text adapted from the Contemporary
English Version, copyright ©1995
American Bible Society
By kind permission of The Bible Society, UK.
Co-edition organised and produced by
Angus Hudson Ltd.,
Concorde House,
Grenville Place,
Mill Hill,
London NW7 3SA
United Kingdom
Tel +44181 959 3668
Fax +44 181 959 3678

Printed in Hong Kong

First published in 1998 by Candle Books
Distributed by SP Valley Ltd,
Triangle Business Park,
Wendover Road, Aylesbury,
Bucks, HP22 5BL, England.

ISBN 1-85985-181-9